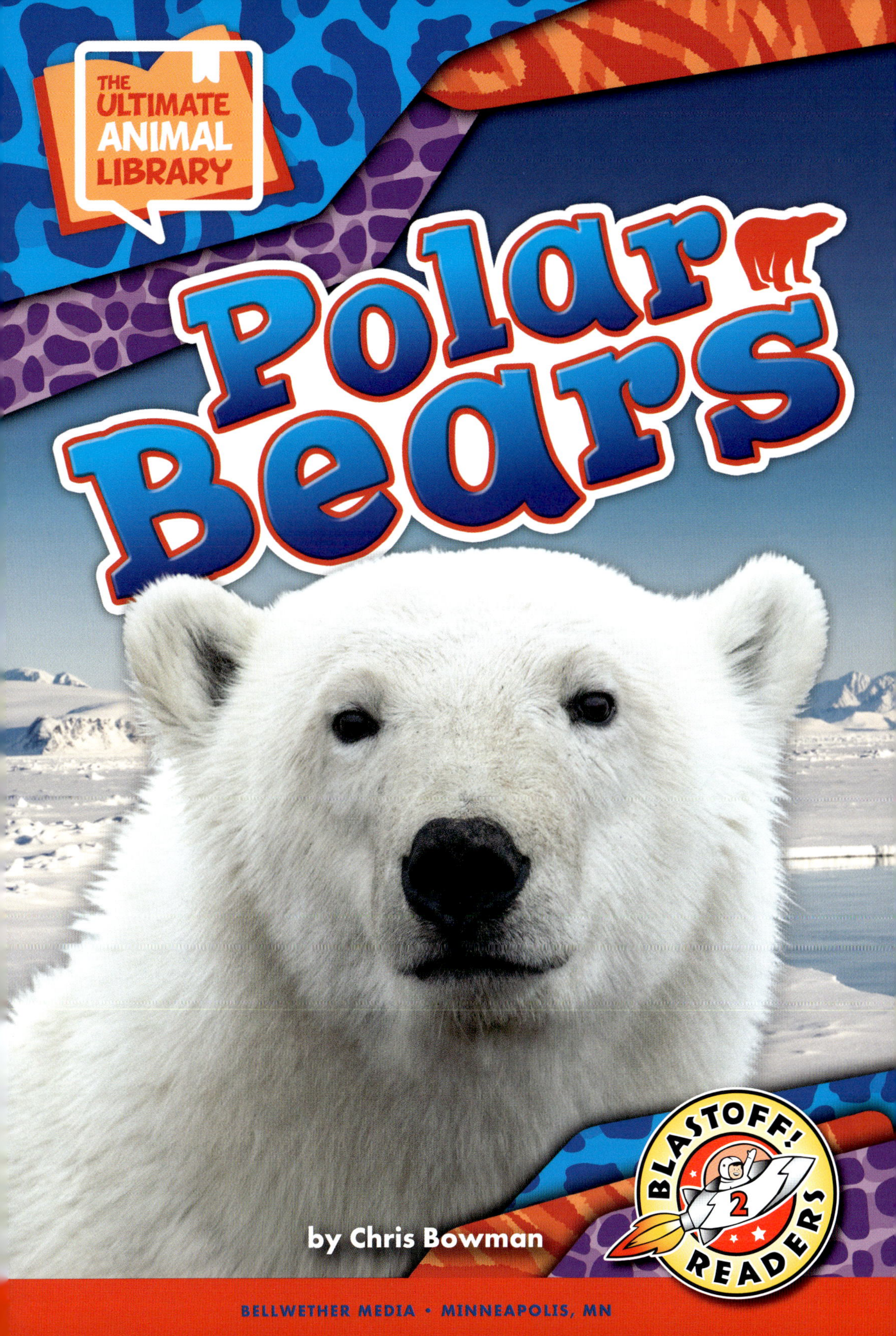
THE ULTIMATE ANIMAL LIBRARY
Polar Bears
by Chris Bowman
BLASTOFF! READERS
2
BELLWETHER MEDIA • MINNEAPOLIS, MN

Blastoff! Readers are carefully developed by literacy experts to build reading stamina and move students toward fluency by combining standards-based content with developmentally appropriate text.

Level 1 provides the most support through repetition of high-frequency words, light text, predictable sentence patterns, and strong visual support.

Level 2 offers early readers a bit more challenge through varied sentences, increased text load, and text-supportive special features.

Level 3 advances early-fluent readers toward fluency through increased text load, less reliance on photos, advancing concepts, longer sentences, and more complex special features.

Reading Level

Grade K

Grades 1–3

Grade 4

This edition first published in 2025 by Bellwether Media, Inc.

Library of Congress Cataloging-in-Publication Data

Names: Bowman, Chris, 1990- author.
Title: Polar bears / by Chris Bowman.
Description: Minneapolis, MN : Bellwether Media Inc., 2025. | Series: Blastoff! Readers: The Ultimate Animal Library | Includes bibliographical references and index. | Audience: Ages 5-8 | Audience: Grades 2-3 | Summary: "Relevant images match informative text in this introduction to polar bears. Intended for students in kindergarten through third grade"-- Provided by publisher.
Identifiers: LCCN 2024038356 (print) | LCCN 2024038357 (ebook) | ISBN 9798893042429 (library binding) | ISBN 9798893043396 (ebook)
Subjects: LCSH: Polar bear--Juvenile literature.
Classification: LCC QL737.C27 B67457 2025 (print) | LCC QL737.C27 (ebook) | DDC 599.786--dc23/eng/20240830
LC record available at https://lccn.loc.gov/2024038356
LC ebook record available at https://lccn.loc.gov/2024038357

Editor: Elizabeth Neuenfeldt Series Designer: Veah Demmin

Printed in the United States of America, North Mankato, MN.

Table of Contents

What Are Polar Bears?

Polar bears are large **mammals**. They are the largest **carnivores** on land! These bears have rounded heads and long necks.

Polar Bear Report

Range

Status in the Wild

Habitat

These bears have
two **coats** of fur.
Their outer **guard hairs**
stick together when wet.

This keeps their thick inner fur dry.

Polar bears have a thick
layer of fat under their fur.
They stay safe from the cold.

Small ears and short tails also help them keep warm.

Large paws help
polar bears swim well.
They also help
polar bears walk on ice.

Hairy paw pads keep
them from slipping.

Spot a Polar Bear
small ears
short tail
large paws

Polar bears live in the **Arctic**.
They mostly live alone.

They spend more time
on land in the summer.
They live on ice
during the winter.

Polar bears hunt a lot. They find seals near cracks in the ice.

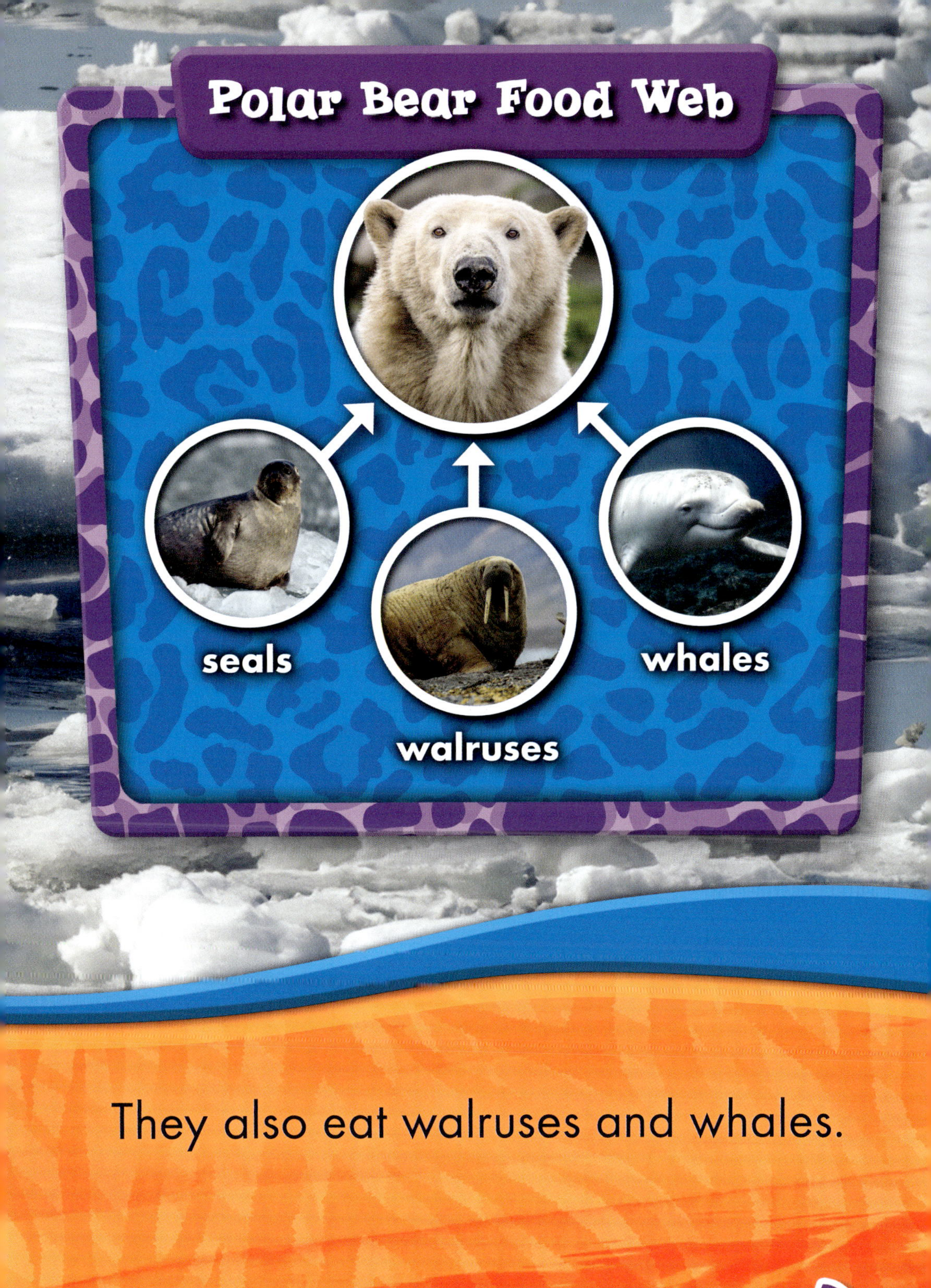

They also eat walruses and whales.

Growing Up

Female polar bears make **dens** when they are **pregnant**.

They make dens in the snow.
They sleep and stay warm.

Females give birth to **cubs** in winter. They have up to three cubs at once.

Cubs only weigh 1 pound (0.5 kilograms) at birth!

Polar bear cubs grow quickly.
Mom teaches them how to hunt.

After two or three years, the cubs can be on their own. Time to search for seals!

Name of Babies

cubs

Number of Babies

up to 3

Time Spent with Mom

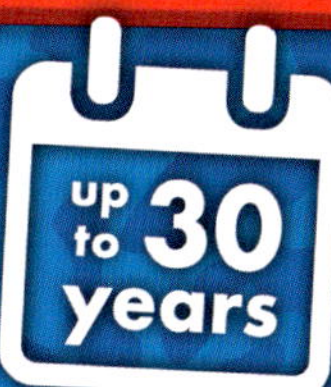

Glossary

Arctic—the cold, frozen land and seas around the North Pole

carnivores—animals that only eat meat

coats—fur or hair covering some animals

cubs—baby polar bears

dens—sheltered places

guard hairs—long, thick hairs on the outside of a polar bear's fur

mammals—warm-blooded animals that have backbones and feed their young milk

pregnant—carrying one or more unborn babies

To Learn More

AT THE LIBRARY

Bowman, Chris. *Grizzly Bears*. Minneapolis, Minn.: Bellwether Media, 2025.

Grack, Rachel. *Polar Bears*. Minneapolis, Minn.: Bellwether Media, 2022.

Schuh, Mari. *Polar Bears*. Minneapolis, Minn.: Jump!, 2022.

ON THE WEB

FACTSURFER

Factsurfer.com gives you a safe, fun way to find more information.

1. Go to www.factsurfer.com.
2. Enter "polar bears" into the search box and click 🔍.
3. Select your book cover to see a list of related content.

Index

The images in this book are reproduced through the courtesy of: James B Williams Photography, front cover; Risto Raunio, front cover background, interior background; krusto, front cover (polar bear icon); ILYA AKINSHIN, p. 3; Vaclav Sebek, p. 4; FloridaStock, pp. 6, 7; Jan_Vondrak, p. 7 (inset); evaurban, pp. 8, 21, 23; Don Landwehrle, p. 9; Henrik Winther Andersen, p. 10; outdoorsman, pp. 10-11; Alexey Seafarer, pp. 11, 19; Steve Allen, p. 12; Vladimir Melnik, p. 13; GTW, pp. 14-15, 20; Jolanda Aalbers, p. 15 (polar bear); Stuedal, p. 15 (walruses); Remo Thommen, p. 15 (seals); RuqayaMai, p. 15 (whales); AndreAnita, p. 16; Sergey Uryadnikov, p. 17; Belovodchenko Anton, p. 18.